River Discoveries

Written by
Ginger Wadsworth

Illustrated by
Paul Kratter

Charlesbridge

Author's Note: Although I was influenced by my favorite river, the Salmon River, my book represents many rivers. Over 75 rivers in North America are 350 or more miles long. The Mississippi, the Yukon, the Missouri, the Snake, the Platte, the Rio Grande, and the Columbia River are just a few. I introduce thirteen water-loving creatures, but there are numerous other animals that live in or near rivers.

In memory of Pete Klinkhammer, river man and baseball fan
—G. W.

To my mother and father
—P. K.

Text copyright © 2002 by Ginger Wadsworth
Illustrations copyright © 2002 by Paul Kratter
All rights reserved, including the right of reproduction in whole or in part in any form. Charlesbridge and colophon are registered trademarks of Charlesbridge Publishing.

Published by Charlesbridge Publishing
85 Main Street
Watertown, MA 02472
(617) 926-0329
www.charlesbridge.com

Illustrations in this book are done in watercolors
Display type and text type set in Sprocket and Tiepolo
Color separations made by Sung In Printing, South Korea
Printed and bound by Sung In Printing, South Korea
Production supervision by Brian G. Walker
Designed by Diane M. Earley

Library of Congress Cataloging-in-Publication Data
Wadsworth, Ginger.
    River discoveries/Ginger Wadsworth; illustrated by Paul Kratter.
        p. cm.
    Summary: Explores the wildlife that depends on a river for food and shelter. Discussion questions follow each section of the text.
    ISBN 1-57091-418-4 (reinforced for library use)
    ISBN 1-57091-419-2 (softcover)
    1. Stream animals—Juvenile literature. 2. Stream animals—Idaho—Salmon River—Juvenile literature. [1. Stream animals.] I. Kratter, Paul, ill. II. Title.
QL145.W34 2002
591.76'4'0979682—dc21   2001004366

Printed in South Korea
(hc) 10 9 8 7 6 5 4 3 2 1
(sc) 10 9 8 7 6 5 4 3 2 1

Water from rain and melting snow runs over rocks and down tiny gullies high in the mountains. These little streams join together to form a river that splashes noisily through canyons. Leaving the mountains, the river widens and slowly winds across open lands. Streams and other rivers flow into the main river all along the way. Hundreds of miles later, it empties into a lake or ocean.

Each watery highway is different, but they all provide a special place where many animals live. Turn the page to discover thirteen animals that depend on this North American river.

Watch for moose along the river in the early morning when the air is still cool. Males, called bulls, have huge, dish-shaped antlers and can weigh 1,600 pounds—as much as a small car. Females, called cows, weigh about 700 to 1,000 pounds. These mammals are vegetarians. They eat about 50 pounds of plants, grasses, bark, or tree branches each day. This hungry male wades into the river and sticks his long head underwater to snack on juicy water plants. He looks up. Stems and roots cling to his antlers and hang from his mouth. He shakes his head, flinging water and plants everywhere. Using his hooves as paddles, the moose swims across the river to find more food. During the heat of the day, he will rest in the shade.

Why are moose called vegetarians?

In the morning, ospreys soar high above the river. These large hawks live near oceans, lakes, and rivers because they eat fish. Ospreys have eyes as powerful as a pair of binoculars. They can see moose grazing along the bank, otters playing in the water, and fish swimming below the surface. Ospreys fly along the river, looking for trout, their favorite kind of fish. This osprey tucks her wings in tight to her body. Whoosh! She dives like a rocket into the river, feet first. Splash! Her razor-sharp talons spear a slippery trout. She lifts off, clutching the wriggling fish, and flies into the sky. Near the river's edge, the osprey joins her mate and two hungry chicks in their nest.

What are these chicks waiting for?

The midmorning sun warms the surface of the water, but brook trout usually stay in deep pools or under large rocks where the water is cool. Colorful layers of skin show through their thin scales, which overlap one another like shingles on a roof. Brook trout are torpedo-shaped so they can swim against the river currents. Their tails and fins help them move forward or turn, stop or stand still. From his watery home, this brook trout watches for the shadowy shapes of ospreys, raccoons, bears, and other fish-eating predators. The fish hovers in place to blend in with the rocks on the river bottom. Oxygen-filled water flows through his mouth and out the gills on the sides of his head. The trout's gills take oxygen from the water. Later, the brook trout will swim to another pool in the river to look for some insects to eat.

How does this trout keep from floating downriver with the currents?

The sun is directly overhead at noon. Shiny water beetles are attracted to the sunlight sparkling on the river. Using their legs like oars, they row through the water. Water beetles are strong swimmers, especially underwater. Before diving, they stick their bottoms out of the water to collect air. The air flows into a special cavity under their hard wings. When beetles are underwater, air moves through tiny tubes from their cavities into their bodies. This beetle zips through the water, right past a hungry trout. She zooms this way and that. Zap! The beetle eats a tadpole. Next she finds a tiny fish. When her air is gone, the beetle races to the river's surface for another breath.

Why is this water beetle like a little rowboat?

If they feel safe during the day, river otters sun themselves beside the river, swim, or play in the water. They find frogs, fish, and other aquatic food to eat. In places where people live along the river, otters tend to be more active at night. These sleek animals are built for life in the water. They have webbed feet, rudderlike tails, and long bodies to help them swim. Dark silky fur insulates them from cold temperatures. River otters love to play. They slide down muddy or snowy riverbanks into the water. They whistle, chatter, and call to one another. Watch this otter push a stick around in the river currents. He does somersaults and dives for pebbles. He even teases a passing beaver by gently pulling its tail. Then the river otter slides onto a rock to enjoy a snack in the warm afternoon sun.

What games do otters play?

Red-winged blackbirds live near the river. They hunt for food, care for their young, and sing to one another all day. In the spring and summer, female blackbirds weave cup-shaped nests near the water. Nests and females are hard to spot in the tall reeds and grasses. The fathers are much easier to see. These shiny black males flash their bright red shoulder patches to scare away hawks, crows, and other predators. They squawk, "check . . . check . . . kong-ka-ree." This new mother has lots to do after her chicks hatch. She searches for fruit, grains, spiders, beetles, and other kinds of insects to feed herself and her babies.

Why does the female have different coloring and markings?

It is dusk along the river. Owls, mountain lions, salamanders, and other nocturnal animals begin to stir. Look for water shrews as they dash in and out of their burrows along the riverbank and squeak at one another. Shrews are tiny mammals that eat their own weight in food each day. You would have to eat at least 200 hamburgers a day to do the same thing! This shrew scurries down a boulder and runs on top of the water for a few seconds. He dives down to grab a dragonfly nymph. Then he pops to the surface like a cork. On the bank, the water shrew fluffs up his fine fur with his back legs. He is still hungry and soon hurries off to find more food.

Where does this water shrew catch some of his food?

Catfish live on the murky river bottom, where they blend in with the rocks, logs, and plants. They can survive in almost any kind of water, hot or cold, fresh or salty or even polluted. Because they do not have good eyesight, catfish have another way of "seeing," especially at night. Whiskers on the sides of their heads, called barbels, have taste buds in them and act as feelers. This hungry catfish swims slowly along the bottom of the river, swinging her head back and forth. Her barbels touch plants and animals, dead and alive. When she feels something, the catfish opens her mouth and sucks in her prey. She swallows everything in one gulp and swims off.

What is this catfish "seeing" with her barbels?

At night, raccoons wake up. They leave their dens in hollow, leaf-lined trees or logs, where they have slept all day. Young cubs go everywhere with their mother. They talk to one another with growls, purrs, twitters, and other sounds. On land, raccoons push aside rocks and poke their long fingers under logs. Because raccoons have a good sense of smell and touch, they can find worms, snails, salamanders, roots, fruit, and other tasty things to eat. This raccoon scurries about, leaving handlike tracks in the mud. He wades into the river to fish for crayfish, tadpoles, or even a slow-moving catfish. His masked face and bushy, ringed tail are easy to see in the moonlight as he jumps from rock to rock.

Where will this raccoon go when the sun comes up?

Tiger salamanders are hard to find during the day. They hide in dark, damp places because the sun dries out their smooth, moist skin. Watch for salamanders when the ground and plants are wet, especially after an evening rain. Salamanders have broad heads, slender bodies, and long tails and toes. These amphibians come in many bright colors and patterns. This salamander crawls out from under a pile of leaves. She cannot hear sounds, like the river flowing nearby, but instead she feels vibrations in the ground. She also has a sharp sense of smell. Both these senses tell the salamander that danger, such as a raccoon, is ahead. She quickly slithers under a log. Later, this tiger salamander will hunt for insects, snails, worms, and even other salamanders to eat.

Why do salamanders like the rain?

Beavers are always busy, especially at night. These big rodents eat bark, twigs, leaves, and roots along the river's edge. Some beavers that live near large rivers or lakes may burrow into the side of a bank to make a den and raise a family. Other beavers live along streams that flow into rivers, and build dams and lodges by cutting down small trees and branches with their teeth. They swim in the river, using their strong, webbed hind feet. A heavy layer of fat and a fur coat keep them from getting cold. This beaver watches and listens for danger. He spots a mountain lion and slaps his tail against the water. Smack! The loud sound warns other beavers to dive underwater or swim to the middle of the river to escape the predator.

Why are the front teeth of a beaver so important?

Mountain lions hunt other animals along the river that are looking for food or coming for a drink of water. These large cats are super athletes. They can jump more than 20 feet, spring from trees, sprint for short distances, and even swim. Mountain lions are also called cougars, catamounts, panthers, or pumas. Males might grow eight feet long from nose to tail and weigh over 200 pounds. Females are about a third smaller. Watch this hungry mountain lion close in on her prey. She pulls in her claws and walks silently on her padded paws. Inch by inch, she creeps forward on her belly. Suddenly she pounces. After a kill, she and her cubs rip off meat with their sharp teeth. Their sandpaper-like tongues clean all the scraps from the bones. When they are full, the mountain lion leads her cubs to a cave or rocky hideaway.

How does this mountain lion sneak up on her prey?

As the sun rises, water shrews, salamanders, beavers, raccoons, and mountain lions go to sleep. Other animals wake up. Moose graze as dragonfly nymphs feed on the river bottom. Nymphs hatch from eggs in the water to slowly develop into dragonflies. This life cycle takes one to five years. Dragonflies are large, winged insects that can fly up to 30 miles an hour. They hover, fly up and down, or dart left and right like miniature helicopters. Iridescent blue, red, orange, yellow, and even purple dragonflies sparkle in the dawn light. This hungry dragonfly's six spindly legs form a perfect bug-collecting basket. The dragonfly can look in nearly every direction for food with its huge eyes. He zooms over the water, scooping up insects in his legs or in his powerful jaws.

What does this dragonfly eat?

How many animals can you find?

Glossary

amphibian: an animal that usually spends its early life in water and later lives both in water and on land.

antlers: bony outgrowths that are usually shed once a year and grow back again.

aquatic: lives in water.

barbels: whiskerlike growths around the mouths of certain fishes.

bull: an adult male of some species.

burrow: a hole or tunnel in the ground dug by an animal for shelter.

cavity: any hollow place.

chick: a young bird.

cow: an adult female of some species.

cub: the young of some species.

dam: something that blocks the flow of water. A beaver dam is made of rocks, dirt, plants, logs, and branches.

den: a cave, hole, or hollow space that an animal uses as a shelter, home, and place to bear young.

fins: thin, winglike flippers on fishes, to help them steer, move, stop, and balance in water.

gills: in fish, a way of taking oxygen from water to breathe.

gully: a small valley worn away by running water.

graze: to feed on grass or plants.

hatch: when young break out of an egg.

hooves: the hard coverings at the end of the toes or feet of certain animals.

insects: small creatures without backbones, having three main body parts, three pairs of legs, and usually two pairs of wings.

insulate: to use fur, feathers, blubber, or other means to protect from cold or heat.

life cycle: from the beginning to the end of life, including reproducing so that new life begins and the cycle continues.

lodge: the shelter, or den, of beavers.

mammals: any group of warm-blooded animals with backbones, including human beings, that feeds its young with milk from the female milk glands.

nocturnal: active at night.

nymph: the young of an insect.

oxygen: a colorless, odorless life supporting element that is about one-fifth of the air.

predator: a plant or animal that hunts and captures another creature for food.

prey: an animal that is hunted for food.

river currents: the direction that water flows in a river.

rodents: small mammals that gnaw and nibble with sharp front teeth that never stop growing.

scales: small, thin protective plates found on some animals' bodies.

species: a group of related plants or animals that can produce young that can also reproduce.

talons: long, sharp claws, especially those belonging to birds.

taste buds: area in the tongue and mouth which detect flavors such as sweet and salty.

territory: an area where an animal lives, usually close to its food source.

vegetarian: an animal that only eats plants and grass.